ZANZIBAR

TRAVEL GUIDE 2024

Ultimate Zanzibar Travel Guide that unveil Zanzibar's Top Attractions, Best Restaurants, Hidden Gems, Beaches, and prepare you for your trip.

Anthony k Raines

All rights reserved. No part of this publication may be reproduced, distributed, or transmitted in any form or by any means, including photocopying, recording, or other electronic or mechanical methods, without the prior written permission of the publisher, except in the case of brief quotations embodied in critical reviews and certain other noncommercial uses permitted by copyright law.

Copyright © Anthony k Raines, 2023.

TABLE OF CONTENT

INTRODUCTION 7

CHAPTER 1....................... 9

History of Zanzibar 9

Geography and Climate 12

CHAPTER 2...................... 16

Getting to Zanzibar 16

Flight Information and Airports............ 16

Sea Routes and Ferries.......................... 19

Visa and Entry Requirements 22

CHAPTER 3 26

Best Time to Visit 26

Seasonal Overview............................... 26

Major Festivals and Events 30

CHAPTER 4.....................34

Culture and People 34

Swahili Traditions and Customs 34

Local Cuisine and Must-Try Dishes 36

Languages Spoken 38

CHAPTER 5 41

Top Attractions 41

Stone Town 41

Beaches of Zanzibar 44

Spice Tours: The Aromatic Experience 47

Jozani Forest 50

CHAPTER 6 54

Accommodations 54

Luxury Resorts and Hotels 54

Budget and Mid-range Stays 58

CHAPTER 7 61

Activities and Adventures 61

Snorkeling and Diving Spots 62

Sailing and Boat Tours 64

CHAPTER 8 68

Local Cuisine and Dining 68

Famous Zanzibari Dishes 69

Top Restaurants and Eateries 72

Street Food and Local Delights 75

CHAPTER 9 79

Souvenirs and Shopping 79

Popular Local Crafts 80

Markets and Shopping Areas 83

CHAPTER 10 87

Nightlife and Entertainment 87

Best Bars and Clubs 87

Cultural Shows and Performances 90

Night Markets 94

CHAPTER 11 97

Getting Around Zanzibar 97

Public Transport Options 97

Car Rentals and Driving Tips 102

Walking and Cycling Paths................. 104

CHAPTER 12...................109

Practical Information 109

Vaccinations and Health Precautions.. 109

Safe Travel Tips................................... 113

Currency and Emergency.................... 117

Conclusion 121

INTRODUCTION

Whisper the name 'Zanzibar' and it instantly evokes images of an island paradise, where azure waters kiss sun-soaked shores, and ancient alleyways tell tales of sultans and spice merchants. This archipelago, nestled off the coast of Tanzania, is more than just a sunbather's retreat; it's a captivating blend of history, culture, and natural beauty.

The Zanzibar Travel Guide is your passport to discovering this enchanting isle in all its facets. From the winding streets of Stone Town, resplendent with its Arabian architecture and UNESCO accolades, to the pristine beaches where time seems to pause, this guide is designed to lead you through every experience and hidden gem. You'll unravel the rich tapestry of Swahili culture, dive into the depths of the Indian Ocean's coral gardens, and indulge in flavors that have been shaped by centuries of trade winds and civilizations.

Whether you're a history enthusiast, a culinary explorer, or simply seeking solace on sandy shores, Zanzibar offers a mosaic of experiences waiting to be unearthed. Let this guide be your compass, leading you to both the famed and the forgotten corners of this island paradise. Welcome to Zanzibar — where every sunset is a story and every wave sings a song of the ages.

CHAPTER 1

History of Zanzibar

Nestled in the warm embrace of the Indian Ocean, the Zanzibar Archipelago has, for centuries, served as a gateway for explorers, traders, and cultures from distant lands. Its history is as vibrant as its waters, marked by a tapestry of influences from Africa, the Middle East, Asia, and Europe.

Ancient Trade Routes:

Long before the era of European exploration, Zanzibar was already a significant node in the maritime trade networks. Arab, Persian, and Indian traders sailed to its shores, enticed by the lucrative trade in spices, ivory, and slaves. These early connections established Zanzibar as an essential hub for commerce and culture in the Indian Ocean.

The Sultanate Era:

The 17th and 18th centuries saw Zanzibar fall under the influence of the Omani Arabs. It was during this period that Stone Town, Zanzibar's historical heart, began to take shape, reflecting the rich Omani architecture. In the mid-19th century, Sultan Seyyid Said moved his capital from Muscat to Zanzibar, further solidifying its status as a significant trading center. Under his rule, the notorious slave trade flourished alongside the spice trade, leading to Zanzibar's moniker as the 'Spice Island'.

The European Influence:

By the late 19th century, European powers began vying for control over parts of Africa. While Zanzibar managed to maintain a degree of autonomy, the British influence was evident. The British took a stand against slavery, leading to its abolition on the islands in 1873. The late 19th and early

20th centuries witnessed a British protectorate over Zanzibar, though it remained under the sultans' nominal rule.

Independence and Union:

The winds of change blew across Africa in the mid-20th century, and Zanzibar was no exception. In 1963, it gained independence from British rule, only to witness a revolution in 1964 that overthrew the sultanate. Later that year, Zanzibar merged with Tanganyika on the mainland to form the United Republic of Tanzania. The union integrated Zanzibar's unique heritage into the larger narrative of the nation, while still preserving its distinct identity.

Today, Zanzibar stands as a testament to its rich history, with every alley in Stone Town and every spice farm echoing tales of its storied past. It remains a melting pot of cultures, an island that has, over the centuries, woven its diverse threads into a vibrant tapestry of history and heritage.

Geography and Climate

Geography:

The Zanzibar Archipelago, located in the Indian Ocean, sits approximately 25-50 kilometers off the eastern coast of Tanzania. The archipelago consists of numerous small islands, but it's predominantly defined by two major islands: Unguja (commonly referred to as Zanzibar Island) and Pemba.

Zanzibar Island, the larger and more developed of the two, houses Stone Town, a UNESCO World Heritage site and the historical heart of Zanzibar. The island's eastern coast is lined with coral reefs and white sandy beaches, while the interior is marked by a verdant landscape of spice plantations, local villages, and patches of tropical forest.

Pemba, to the north of Unguja, is hillier and more lush. It's renowned for its clove production and boasts dense forests and deep lagoons, making it a haven for divers.

Climate:
Zanzibar experiences a tropical coastal climate, characterized by warm weather year-round, punctuated by two main rainy seasons.

Hot Season (December to March): These months are the hottest and most humid, with temperatures often rising above 30°C (86°F). While rain is infrequent during this period, it's not uncommon to experience short, intense rain showers.

Long Rains (Masika) (April to May): This period is the primary rainy season, with long and heavy rainfall. While the landscape becomes lush and vibrant, some regions might experience flooding. Many visitors avoid traveling during this season due to the unpredictability of the rains.

Cool Season (June to October): The temperatures during these months are milder, hovering around 25°C (77°F). With cooler breezes and minimal rainfall, this period is considered the best time to visit the islands.

Short Rains (Vuli) (November): Zanzibar experiences another, albeit shorter, rainy season during November. The rains are less intense compared to the Masika and don't last long.

Despite its tropical climate, Zanzibar benefits from the sea breezes, which temper the heat, making the weather relatively pleasant. For beachgoers and water enthusiasts, the ocean temperature remains inviting throughout the year, averaging between 25°C to 29°C (77°F to 84°F).

In summary, Zanzibar's blend of idyllic beaches, tropical interiors, and diverse climate patterns makes it a unique destination, offering different experiences throughout the year. Whether you're chasing the sun or seeking the cool embrace of the ocean breezes, Zanzibar beckons with its ever-changing moods.

CHAPTER 2

Getting to Zanzibar

Zanzibar, the shimmering jewel of the Indian Ocean, beckons travelers from all over the world with its paradisiacal beaches and rich history. But how does one get to this island oasis? Here's a comprehensive guide to pave the way for your journey to the Spice Island.

Flight Information and Airports

Abeid Amani Karume International Airport (ZNZ)

Zanzibar's primary gateway for international and domestic flights is the Abeid Amani Karume International Airport, located just a short drive from Stone Town, the historic heart of the island. Here's what you need to know:

1. Airlines and Destinations:

International Flights:
- Qatar Airways: Provides connections from Doha.
- Turkish Airlines: Connects Istanbul with Zanzibar.
- FlyDubai: Services between Dubai and Zanzibar.
- Ethiopian Airlines: Flights from Addis Ababa.
- Other carriers include Oman Air (from Muscat), Kenya Airways (from Nairobi), and Condor (from Frankfurt), among others.

Domestic and Regional Flights:
- Precision Air, Air Tanzania, and Fastjet: Frequent daily flights connecting Zanzibar with Dar es Salaam, Tanzania's primary hub.
- Coastal Aviation: Offers charter flights and scheduled services to several destinations within Tanzania, including Arusha, Serengeti, Selous, and more.
- Auric Air: Connects Zanzibar with Pemba Island and several other regional destinations.

2. Facilities:

The airport, while not large, offers essential facilities to cater to international and domestic travelers:

- Currency Exchange: There are bureaus for converting foreign currency.
- Shops: A few duty-free stores and local souvenir shops.
- Dining: Some small cafés and snack bars.
- Transport: Taxis are available for transfer to Stone Town and other parts of the island. Pre-booking transportation with hotels or tour operators is also common.

3. Tips and Considerations:

1. Transit: Travelers with layovers should note that the airport is compact with limited amenities for long waits. It's advisable to check transit visa requirements if considering leaving the airport.
2. Health: Depending on your origin, you may be required to show proof of yellow fever vaccination upon arrival.

3. Customs and Immigration: As with any international travel, ensure you have all the necessary documents, including visas (if required), for a smooth entry process. Zanzibar follows Tanzanian visa and immigration rules.
4. Connectivity: While the majority of travelers arrive at Zanzibar directly from international locations, many opt for a two-step journey, first landing in Dar es Salaam (Julius Nyerere International Airport) and then taking a short domestic flight to Zanzibar.

While Zanzibar's airport might not be grand in scale, it serves as a welcoming portal to the island's myriad of experiences. With the scent of spices in the air and the promise of adventure ahead, your journey begins the moment you touch down.

Sea Routes and Ferries

Zanzibar, with its strategic location in the Indian Ocean, has historically been a significant maritime hub. Today, it remains accessible by sea, offering travelers an alternative and scenic mode of reaching the island.

1. from Dar es Salaam to Zanzibar:
- Dar es Salaam, Tanzania's bustling coastal city, is the primary ferry gateway to Zanzibar.
- Azam Marine & Coastal Fast Ferries: One of the most prominent and reputable operators, they offer multiple daily trips between Dar es Salaam and Zanzibar. The journey on their modern vessels, equipped with air conditioning and entertainment, usually takes about 2 hours.
- Zanzibar Fast Ferries: Another reliable operator, their boat, the Kilimanjaro, is well-maintained and offers comfortable seating options ranging from economy to VIP.

2. from Pemba Island to Zanzibar:

Pemba Island, Zanzibar's sister island to the north, also has ferry connections to Zanzibar, though they are less frequent and might be a bit more rustic in experience.

3. Safety and Booking Tips:

- Book directly or Through Reputable Agents: To ensure authenticity and avoid overpaying, it's best to book your ticket directly at the ferry company's office or through recognized travel agencies. Be cautious of touts or unofficial agents who might approach you with offers.
- Timings: While ferries operate at various times throughout the day, morning departures are popular among tourists, as they allow a full day of exploration upon arrival.
- Luggage: Most ferries have a luggage hold. Ensure your bags are tagged, and keep your valuables with you.
- Seasickness: The Indian Ocean can be a bit choppy, especially during the monsoon seasons. If you're prone to seasickness, consider taking preventive measures.

- Arrival: Upon reaching Zanzibar, you'll disembark at the Stone Town ferry terminal. From here, you can easily find taxis or arrange transport to your hotel.

4. Views and Experience:
Traveling by sea to Zanzibar offers a unique experience. As the Dar es Salaam skyline fades, the vast expanse of the Indian Ocean surrounds you, culminating in the first glimpse of Zanzibar's shores, with the spires of Stone Town and the scent of cloves heralding your arrival.

In essence, while flying is quick and convenient, taking the sea route to Zanzibar is an experience in itself, intertwining the thrill of voyage with the promise of the adventures awaiting on the island.

Visa and Entry Requirements

While Zanzibar is part of Tanzania, its island location necessitates some specific considerations for travelers. Here's a comprehensive breakdown of the visa and entry requirements for Zanzibar:

1. Visa Requirements:

- Visa On Arrival: For many nationalities, visas can be obtained upon arrival at Abeid Amani Karume International Airport in Zanzibar or at any other official Tanzanian entry point. The standard visa fee for most countries is $50, but it's $100 for US citizens. The visa is typically valid for 90 days.
- E-Visa: Tanzania introduced an e-Visa system, allowing travelers to apply for and receive their visa electronically before departure. It's a convenient method that can save time upon arrival.
- Exemptions: Some nationalities, primarily from African and Commonwealth countries, are exempt from Tanzanian visa requirements. However, this list can change, so it's always good to check the latest updates.

2. Passport Validity:

Travelers must have a passport valid for at least six months from the date of entry into Zanzibar/Tanzania.

3. Yellow Fever Vaccination:

If you're arriving from or transiting through a country with a risk of yellow fever transmission, you're required to present a valid yellow fever vaccination certificate upon entry. This is especially important for travelers from neighboring East and Central African countries or South America.

4. Other Vaccinations and Health Considerations:

While not mandatory, it's recommended for travelers to consider vaccinations for typhoid, hepatitis A and B, and cholera. Taking malaria prophylaxis is also advisable due to the presence of the disease in the region.

5. Proof of Onward Travel:

While not always enforced, officials might request evidence of onward travel, be it a return ticket or a ticket to another destination.

6. Local Registration:

If you're staying in Zanzibar for more than 3 days, you're required to register at a local police station. However, most hotels and accommodations will handle this registration on behalf of their guests.

7. Additional Considerations for Zanzibar:

While Zanzibar follows Tanzania's visa and entry regulations, the island has additional checkpoints upon arrival and departure. Ensure you keep your passport and any other relevant documents handy.

While Zanzibar is fairly welcoming and accessible to international travelers, it's essential to plan ahead and ensure all visa and health requirements are met. This will ensure a smooth and hassle-free entry, allowing you to dive right into the wonders that this island paradise has to offer.

CHAPTER 3

Best Time to Visit

Choosing the right time to visit Zanzibar can significantly enhance your experience on this idyllic island. The archipelago's location near the equator means it has a tropical climate, but there are certain periods that stand out for their optimal travel conditions. Here's a guide to help you pinpoint the best time for your Zanzibari adventure.

Seasonal Overview

Zanzibar's equatorial location gifts it with a tropical climate, resulting in distinct seasonal variations that influence travel experiences. Here's a snapshot of what each season offers, ensuring you align your travel plans with the island's rhythm.

1. Cool and Dry Season (June to October):
- Weather: Characterized by clear blue skies, comfortable temperatures averaging around 25°C (77°F), and minimal rainfall. The cool ocean breezes make this period particularly pleasant for sunbathing, swimming, and outdoor activities.
- Tourism: This is a popular time for travelers, and you can expect busier beaches and higher hotel occupancy, especially in prime locations.

2. Hot and Dry Season (December to February):
- Weather: As the name suggests, this is when the island experiences its highest temperatures, sometimes going beyond 30°C (86°F). The weather is hot and dry, with occasional short-lived rain showers.
- Tourism: Being a peak travel season, especially around the December holidays, expect a bustling atmosphere in

tourist hotspots. It's a great time for underwater activities due to clear water visibility.

3. Long Rains (April to May):

- Weather: Known as 'Masika', this is the main rainy season for Zanzibar. The island witnesses long, heavy rainfall, interspersed with sunny intervals. The landscape turns lush and vibrant, but some areas might experience flooding.
- Tourism: Due to the unpredictable weather, fewer tourists visit during these months. However, this means fewer crowds, lower prices, and a more serene atmosphere. It's an ideal time for those seeking tranquillity, but some resorts might close during this period for maintenance.

4. Short Rains (November):

- Weather: Termed 'Vuli', this short rainy season brings sporadic and lighter rain showers compared to the Masika period. The rains are usually in the form of short, intense bursts, followed by sunshine.

- Tourism: Tourist numbers begin to pick up as the short rains rarely disrupt activities. The mix of rain-refreshed landscapes and sunny spells offers a unique ambiance.

5. Transition Periods (March and November):
- Weather: March sees the transition from the hot season to the long rains, while late November marks the shift from short rains to the hot season. These months have variable weather patterns but generally provide a mix of sun and light rain.
- Tourism: As transitional months, they can offer a balanced experience of good weather and moderate tourist numbers.

Your ideal time to visit Zanzibar depends on your preferences. Whether you're chasing the sun, seeking off-peak tranquillity, or wish to experience the island's refreshed beauty after the rains, Zanzibar promises a memorable experience. Always remember to check specific events or festivals when planning, as these can also influence the best times to visit

Major Festivals and Events

The rich tapestry of cultures in Zanzibar has given birth to a vibrant calendar of festivals and events. These gatherings celebrate the island's unique blend of African, Arab, European, and Indian influences, offering visitors a deeper insight into its history and traditions.

1. Zanzibar International Film Festival (ZIFF) (July):
- Description: Often termed as the "Festival of the Dhow Countries", ZIFF is East Africa's largest film, music, and arts festival. The festival screens films from all over the world, with a special emphasis on Swahili-speaking regions.
- Highlights: Film screenings, music performances, workshops, exhibitions, and the famous Dhow Race.

2. Sauti za Busara (February):
- Description: A renowned music festival that translates to "Sounds of Wisdom", it brings together artists from across the African continent.
- Highlights: Live music performances, traditional dances, and vibrant parades through Stone Town.

3. Eid Celebrations (Date varies based on the Islamic lunar calendar):

- Description: As a predominantly Muslim region, Zanzibar celebrates the two Eid festivals with fervor - Eid al-Fitr marking the end of Ramadan and Eid al-Adha commemorating Abraham's willingness to sacrifice his son.
- Highlights: Feasting, prayers, traditional dances, and music.

4. Zanzibar Beach & Watersports Festival (September):

- Description: Celebrated on Jambiani Beach, this festival is a treat for beach lovers and watersports enthusiasts.
- Highlights: Kite surfing, beach soccer, traditional boat racing, music, dance, and local food stalls.

5. Spice Festival (Date varies):

- Description: Celebrating Zanzibar's title as the "Spice Island", this festival delves into the world of spices, from their cultivation to their culinary and medicinal uses.

- Highlights: Spice tours, cooking classes, workshops, and a spice market.

6. Maulidi Festival (Date varies based on the Islamic lunar calendar):

- Description: This religious festival marks the birth of Prophet Muhammad. It's particularly vibrant in Zanzibar due to the island's significant Islamic influence.
- Highlights: Processions, readings from the Quran, traditional dances, and feasts.

7. Nguvumali Festival (October):

- Description: An event dedicated to promoting environmental awareness and conservation in Zanzibar.
- Highlights: Beach clean-ups, environmental workshops, music, and dance performances.

8. Zanzibar Cultural Festival (July):

- Description: This festival celebrates the rich and diverse cultural heritage of Zanzibar.

- Highlights: Traditional music and dance performances, arts and crafts exhibitions, and local culinary showcases.

Attending one of Zanzibar's festivals or events provides an unparalleled opportunity to immerse oneself in the island's soul. It's a chance to experience Zanzibar beyond its beaches, diving deep into its traditions, stories, and rhythms. If your travel dates are flexible, aligning your visit with one of these occasions can greatly enrich your Zanzibari experience.

CHAPTER 4

Culture and People

Zanzibar, often referred to as the "Spice Island", is not just a geographical marvel but a cultural melting pot, where centuries of trade, migration, and conquest have shaped a distinct and diverse society.

Swahili Traditions and Customs

Zanzibar, an island shimmering off the Tanzanian coast, is a living testament to the Swahili culture, a confluence of African, Arab, Persian, and Indian influences. The iconic wooden boats with triangular sails, known as dhows, exemplify the Swahili people's deep connection to the ocean. They have historically been pivotal for trade, fishing, and travel, and even today, traditional dhow building using age-old techniques remains a cherished craft. The island's architecture further reflects its Swahili heritage, with houses in Stone Town showcasing carved wooden doors, internal courtyards, and verandas. These homes often feature "baraza" – stone benches where residents and passersby exchange tales and daily news.

Celebrations are central to Swahili life in Zanzibar. Multi-day wedding ceremonies are marked by various rituals, including the "kichanga," where brides adorn their hands and feet with intricate henna patterns. As the ceremonies unfold, the rhythmic beats of Taarab music, a unique blend of Middle Eastern, Indian, and African tunes, often resonate in the background. This musical tradition uses instruments like the "oud" and "qanun", and its lyrics weave stories of love, societal observations, and more.

Language, too, plays a significant role in Swahili culture. Swahili, enriched with proverbs, riddles, and poetry, has historically been a medium for poets to advise rulers, opine on societal matters, or simply share tales of romance. The island's attire, marked by women's vibrant "kanga" or "kitenge" and men's "kanzus", mirrors the blend of modesty and flair inherent to Swahili culture. Food, influenced by the island's "Spice Island" moniker, brings together coconut, fish, rice, and an array of spices in dishes like "biryani" and "samosas".

Religion, predominantly Islam, guides many of Zanzibar's festivities. Celebrations like Eid al-Fitr and Eid al-Adha see prayers, feasting, and acts of charity. Beyond the observable traditions, the Swahili in Zanzibar also deeply value their indigenous knowledge systems, including traditional medicine. Local healers or "mgangas" often prescribe remedies crafted from herbs, roots, and spices, upholding a legacy of natural healing passed down through generations. In essence, the Swahili traditions and customs of Zanzibar offer a mesmerizing blend of histories and cultures, making it a treasure trove of experiences for every visitor.

Local Cuisine and Must-Try Dishes

Zanzibar, fondly referred to as the "Spice Island", boasts a culinary landscape as diverse as its history. Influenced by Bantu, Arab, Indian, and European palates, the island's cuisine offers a delightful fusion of flavors, techniques, and ingredients. Here's a taste of the local cuisine and some must-try dishes:

1. Biryani and Pilau: Borrowed from Indian and Persian culinary traditions but with a distinct Swahili twist,

these are flavorful rice dishes often served with chicken, beef, or seafood. While Biryani is layered with meat and rice, Pilau is a spiced rice often cooked with meat or fish infused with spices like cloves, cumin, and cardamom.

2. Urojo Soup: Commonly known as "Zanzibar Mix", this is a tangy, spicy street food staple. It's a soup made with a mix of beans, potatoes, fried bhajias, and sometimes meat or fish, drenched in a tangy mango-based sauce, topped with peanuts and crispy fried potato shavings.
3. Octopus Curry: A testament to the island's rich marine resources, this dish features tender octopus cooked in a creamy, spicy coconut sauce.
4. Mandazi: A popular breakfast item or snack, these are Swahili doughnuts. They're slightly sweet, spiced with cardamom, and deep-fried to golden perfection.
5. Zanzibari Pizza: Unlike any traditional pizza, this local favorite consists of a thin dough filled with a mix of ingredients like meat, chicken, seafood, vegetables, and even sweet fillings like chocolate and banana. It's folded into a square or circle and fried until crispy.

6. Samaki wa Kupaka: Fresh fish, often grilled to perfection, slathered in a rich coconut sauce spiced with turmeric, garlic, and chili. It's a delightful representation of Zanzibar's coastal flavors.
7. Chapati: Influenced by Indian flatbreads, the Swahili version is slightly thicker and is often enjoyed with curries or used to scoop up beans or stews.
8. Mishkaki: These are skewered and grilled meat chunks similar to kebabs, marinated in spices and often served with sides of vegetables or rice.
9. Wali na Maharage: A simple yet staple dish, it comprises rice served with a flavorful bean stew cooked in coconut milk and spices.
10. Tropical Fruits and Juices: Given its equatorial location, Zanzibar is home to a plethora of fresh tropical fruits like coconuts, mangoes, jackfruits, and passion fruits. Fresh fruit juices and smoothies are widely available and are a must-try, especially the tangy "baobab juice".

Languages Spoken

Zanzibar, with its intricate tapestry of cultures and histories, is a linguistic hub that has witnessed the confluence of various tongues. The predominant and official language of Zanzibar is Swahili (or Kiswahili). Originating from the Bantu languages, Swahili has absorbed words and phrases from various languages due to trade and migrations over the centuries, including Arabic, Persian, English, Portuguese, and German. It serves not only as the lingua franca of Zanzibar but also of much of East Africa. Most Zanzibaris speak Swahili as their first language and use it in daily interactions, business, education, and government.

In addition to Swahili, English is widely spoken, especially in the tourism sector, government functions, and higher education. It's not uncommon to find locals, particularly in the tourism industry, conversing fluently in English.

Given Zanzibar's historical ties with Oman and other parts of the Arab world, Arabic is also spoken, especially among the older generation and those involved in religious scholarship.

Furthermore, due to the influence of Indian and Pakistani traders and immigrants, you'll find a minority of Zanzibaris who can speak Gujarati or other South Asian languages.

While Swahili remains the heart of linguistic expression in Zanzibar, the echoes of the island's diverse past and cosmopolitan spirit can be heard in the variety of languages spoken by its residents.

CHAPTER 5

Top Attractions

Zanzibar, often dubbed the "Spice Island", is a paradise filled with attractions that cater to history enthusiasts, beach lovers, and cultural explorers alike. Here are some of the top attractions that Zanzibar offers

Stone Town

Stone Town, the ancient heart of Zanzibar, stands as a living testament to the island's storied past, a confluence of African, Arab, Indian, and European influences. Recognized as a UNESCO World Heritage Site, it beckons visitors with its labyrinthine alleys, grand old Arabian homes, ornate palaces, and historic mosques. Each corner of this old town whispers tales of sultans, slaves, and explorers, all of whom have left an indelible mark on its fabric.

Central to Stone Town's character are its intricately carved wooden doors, many adorned with brass studs, serving as silent witnesses to the prosperity and significance of their former owners. These doors, influenced by various architectural styles, give a glimpse into the town's multicultural heritage.

The House of Wonders, locally known as Beit al Ajaib, stands tall among Stone Town's buildings. Once the grand palace of the Sultan of Zanzibar, it was one of the first buildings in East Africa to have electricity. Its large clock tower and broad balconies offer panoramic views of the town and the shimmering Indian Ocean beyond.

Not far from the House of Wonders is the Old Fort. Built in the late 17th century, it's the oldest building in Stone Town. Over the years, it has served various roles, from a defense fortification to a prison, and now as a cultural center, hosting art exhibitions, workshops, and concerts.

Stone Town's past also holds a somber chapter. The former slave market stands as a poignant reminder of the dark times when Zanzibar was at the epicenter of the East African slave trade. The Anglican Cathedral, built on the site of the old slave market, now memorializes the abolition of slavery, with its altar standing on the exact spot of the former whipping post.

The town's bustling marketplaces are a sensory delight. From the vibrant Darajani Market, filled with spices, fresh produce, and seafood, to the numerous curio shops selling crafts, antiques, and textiles, shopping in Stone Town is an experience in itself.

As day turns to night, the Forodhani Gardens come alive. Overlooking the harbor, this nighttime food market is a haven for gourmets, offering everything from freshly grilled seafood to local delicacies.

Walking through Stone Town is akin to traveling back in time. Its mosaic of cultures, rich history, and architectural marvels make it not just a place on a map, but a journey through centuries, a tale of an island that became a melting pot of civilizations.

Beaches of Zanzibar

Zanzibar, an archipelago nestled in the Indian Ocean, is famed not just for its rich history and culture but also for its idyllic beaches. These sun-kissed shores, with their soft white sands, azure waters, and lush palm trees, offer a tropical haven for beach lovers and water sports enthusiasts alike. Here's a comprehensive guide to the beaches of Zanzibar:

Nungwi Beach: Located on the northern tip of the island, Nungwi is known for its postcard-perfect vistas and vibrant sunsets. The beach remains tidal independent, ensuring constant access to its crystal-clear waters. With a selection of beach bars and restaurants, Nungwi also provides a bustling nightlife.

Kendwa Beach: Adjacent to Nungwi, Kendwa offers a slightly more relaxed ambiance. Famous for its monthly full moon parties, Kendwa is the place for those looking to combine tranquility with occasional festivities.

Paje Beach: On the east coast, Paje is a magnet for watersports enthusiasts, particularly kite surfers. The strong, consistent winds and shallow waters create ideal conditions for kite surfing, making Paje a renowned spot for this thrilling sport.

Jambiani Beach: Stretching along the southeast coast, Jambiani is characterized by its traditional wooden fishing boats and coral reefs. The village nearby gives travelers an insight into the local life, with seaweed farming being a common sight.

Bwejuu Beach: This beach is often listed among Africa's best beaches. Bwejuu offers a serene environment, perfect for relaxation and taking in the island's natural beauty.

Mnemba Island: A short boat ride from the northeast coast of Zanzibar, Mnemba Island boasts a private atoll. It's a diver's paradise, with its surrounding coral reefs teeming with marine life, from colorful fish to turtles.

Dongwe Beach: Closer to the southern tip, Dongwe stands at the edge of the Michamvi Peninsula. Its turquoise waters and wide stretch of white sands make it an excellent choice for sunbathing and swimming.

Pingwe Beach: Famous for the iconic "The Rock" restaurant, which stands on a rock just offshore, Pingwe is a delightful blend of scenic beauty and culinary allure.

Kizimkazi Beach: Located in the south, Kizimkazi is renowned for its dolphin tours. The bay is home to several pods of dolphins, and early morning boat tours offer the chance to spot and even swim with these playful creatures.

Michamvi Beach: This is a crescent-shaped beach on the Michamvi Peninsula, offering visitors breathtaking sunsets and a chance to explore the nearby mangrove forest.

Zanzibar's beaches are more than just stretches of sand. They are gateways to unique experiences, be it adventurous water sports, insights into local life, or simple, unadulterated relaxation. Each beach, with its distinctive charm, ensures that every visitor finds their slice of paradise on the "Spice Island."

Spice Tours: The Aromatic Experience

Zanzibar, often heralded as the "Spice Island", has a legacy deeply intertwined with spices. From the days of the Omani Sultans to the present, the island has been a hub for the cultivation and trade of a variety of aromatic and flavorful spices. The spice tours of Zanzibar offer an immersive experience into this fragrant world, transporting visitors from the bustling markets of Stone Town to the verdant spice farms that dot the island's landscape.

As one embarks on a spice tour, the first thing that strikes is the sheer abundance. Cloves, nutmeg, cardamom, vanilla, cinnamon, black pepper, and turmeric are just some of the spices that thrive in Zanzibar's tropical climate. Walking through these farms is an exploration not just of sight, but of all senses. The air is thick with mixed aromas, each spice offering its distinct note.

Guides, well-versed in both the history and uses of each spice, pluck fresh pods, roots, and barks, encouraging visitors to guess them by their aroma. Touching, tasting, and smelling these spices in their raw form is a revelation, a far cry from the packaged versions found in supermarket shelves.

The spice tour isn't just about the spices in their grown form but also delves into their journey from farm to table. Traditional processing methods, such as sun drying cloves or grinding turmeric, are demonstrated. Visitors also learn about the medicinal, cosmetic, and culinary applications of each spice. Did you know, for instance, that nutmeg, beyond its culinary use, was once highly valued for its supposed medicinal properties, or that the oil extracted from ylang-ylang flowers is a key ingredient in many perfumes?

No spice tour in Zanzibar is complete without a meal. Many tours culminate in a traditional Swahili lunch or dinner, where dishes infused with the day's highlighted spices are served, offering a tangible (and delectable) culmination to the aromatic journey.

Moreover, many spice farms also produce and sell a range of products, from pure spice packets to cosmetics and perfumes. These make for perfect souvenirs, allowing one to take a piece of Zanzibar's fragrant heart back home.

In essence, Zanzibar's spice tours are not just an excursion but an aromatic voyage through time. They narrate tales of sultans and traders, of ancient maritime routes, and of an island whose history and culture have been shaped profoundly by these magical condiments. For any visitor to Zanzibar, this aromatic experience is truly unmissable.

Jozani Forest

Tucked away in the heart of Zanzibar is the Jozani Forest, a verdant expanse that stands in contrast to the island's sun-kissed beaches. A visit to Jozani offers a refreshing foray into a tropical paradise, but what truly sets this forest apart is its most famed resident: the endangered Red Colobus Monkey.

This species, endemic to Zanzibar, finds its last remaining refuge in the Jozani Forest. With a population of only a few thousand, the Red Colobus Monkey is one of Africa's rarest primates. Recognizable by its distinct reddish coat, tufted white hair, and black face, this primate is both playful and curious, making it a delight for visitors to observe.

Jozani Forest, spread across 50 square kilometers, forms part of the larger Jozani Chwaka Bay National Park. The forest is a mosaic of diverse habitats, from mangrove swamps and salt marshes to dense thickets and woodland. This varied environment not only supports the Red Colobus Monkey but also plays host to a myriad of other wildlife species, including the Sykes monkey, bushbabies, and over 40 species of birds.

A walk through the forest, often on wooden boardwalks that meander through the mangroves, is an immersive experience. The air is filled with the calls of birds, the rustling of leaves, and, if you're lucky, the playful chatters of the Red Colobus troops. Apart from the monkeys, it's not uncommon to spot vibrant butterflies flitting around, or even the occasional shy chameleon blending into the foliage.

The local community plays an integral role in conserving Jozani Forest and its inhabitants. Conservation efforts are bolstered by the employment and training of local guides, who possess an intimate knowledge of the forest's secrets. These guides not only lead visitors through designated trails but also share insights into the delicate balance of the ecosystem, the behaviors of the Red Colobus Monkey, and the ongoing conservation initiatives.

Jozani Forest isn't merely a tourist attraction; it's a testament to Zanzibar's commitment to preserving its natural treasures. The forest stands as a sanctuary where the delicate balance between humans and nature is maintained and celebrated.

For anyone visiting Zanzibar, a trip to Jozani Forest offers a rare opportunity to come face-to-face with the enchanting Red Colobus Monkey and to appreciate the island's rich biodiversity. Beyond the pristine beaches and historical alleys of Stone Town, Jozani is a reminder of the wild, untamed beauty that Zanzibar harbors within its heart.

CHAPTER 6

Accommodations

Finding the perfect place to rest one's head after a day of exploring is an essential part of any traveler's itinerary, and Zanzibar does not disappoint. The island offers a range of accommodations to suit every taste and budget, from luxurious beachfront resorts to charming boutique hotels and cozy guesthouses.

Luxury Resorts and Hotels

Nestled in the shimmering waters of the Indian Ocean, Zanzibar has, over the years, transformed into a luxurious retreat that seamlessly merges its rich history and vibrant culture with contemporary luxury. This island paradise is home to a plethora of luxury resorts and hotels, each offering a slice of tropical opulence against the backdrop of Zanzibar's stunning landscapes. Let's delve into some of the most exquisite accommodations this "Spice Island" has to offer.

Zuri Zanzibar: Overlooking the turquoise waters of Kendwa Beach, Zuri Zanzibar offers a blend of stylish design and lush surroundings. With a focus on sustainability and local craftsmanship, this resort boasts bungalows, suites, and villas that come with private terraces and beach access. The property's vast spice gardens, infinity pool, and diverse dining options make it a top choice for those seeking a modern luxury experience.

Constance Aiyana: Located in Pemba Island, part of the Zanzibar Archipelago, Constance Aiyana is the epitome of serene luxury. With its coral limestone villas facing the azure sea, the resort offers a harmonious blend of luxury and nature. The spa, using only organic products, provides holistic wellness experiences for the discerning traveler.

The Residence Zanzibar: Nestled amidst 32 hectares of tropical gardens, The Residence Zanzibar offers luxurious villas with private pools. Combining contemporary design with Swahili accents, this resort ensures privacy and world-class amenities. Its glass-bottom boat rides, spa village, and array of dining options make it a sought-after luxury destination.

Park Hyatt Zanzibar: Situated in the heart of historic Stone Town, Park Hyatt offers a luxurious take on Zanzibar's rich heritage. With views of the dhow harbor and the Indian Ocean, the hotel seamlessly blends modern comforts with the island's Swahili architecture. The Anantara Spa and the Dining Room restaurant are just a couple of the many offerings that cater to guests seeking elegance and refinement.

Breezes Beach Club & Spa: Located on the pristine Bwejuu-Paje beach, this resort is a haven for those looking to experience luxury in an intimate setting. Known for its personalized service, the property boasts rooms adorned with hand-carved Zanzibari furniture, four-poster beds, and expansive views of the ocean.

Baraza Resort & Spa: Channeling the opulence of the sultans and days gone by, Baraza Resort & Spa offers villas adorned with intricate Swahili designs. From its thalassotherapy treatments in the Frangipani Spa to the culinary delights in its restaurants, every aspect of this resort is curated for luxury.

Zanzibar's luxury resorts and hotels provide a haven where the island's rich tapestry of cultures, histories, and landscapes meet modern opulence. Whether you're lounging in a private pool overlooking the ocean, tasting gourmet dishes infused with local spices, or exploring the historic lanes of Stone Town, Zanzibar's luxury accommodations ensure an experience that is both unparalleled and unforgettable.

Budget and Mid-range Stays

Zanzibar, an enchanting island off the coast of Tanzania, offers a kaleidoscope of experiences. While it's home to several luxury resorts, travelers on a budget or those seeking mid-range options need not fret. The island boasts a plethora of accommodations that are both wallet-friendly and rich in character.

Budget Stays in Zanzibar:

Zanzibar White Sand Hostel: Perfect for backpackers and solo travelers, this hostel in Stone Town provides clean rooms, communal spaces for mingling, and is a stone's throw away from major attractions.

Amaan Nungwi Hostel: Located near the popular Nungwi Beach, Amaan offers budget-friendly rooms and dormitories. It's a great base for those keen on exploring the beach, with local eateries and activities nearby.

Jambo Brothers Bungalows: Situated in Jambiani, these bungalows offer basic amenities amidst a tranquil setting.

The beachfront location and the warm hospitality of the hosts ensure a pleasant stay.

Mid-range Stays in Zanzibar:

Tembo House Hotel & Apartments: Located in Stone Town, this historic building offers a blend of Swahili architecture and modern comfort. The sea-facing rooms, an inviting pool, and an in-house restaurant make it a favorite among mid-range travelers.

Mangrove Lodge: Nestled amidst mangroves and palm trees, this eco-friendly lodge in Chuini provides well-equipped bungalows with a touch of Zanzibari decor. The serene environment, coupled with activities like canoeing and village tours, offers a wholesome experience.

Kichanga Lodge: Perched on the southeast coast in Michamvi, Kichanga offers beachfront bungalows and villas. With a focus on sustainability, the lodge boasts a relaxed ambiance, making it perfect for those seeking to unwind.

Uroa Bay Beach Resort: Located on Uroa Beach, this mid-range resort offers spacious rooms, a sizable pool, and multiple dining options. It provides a balanced blend of leisure activities and relaxation opportunities.

Zanzibar Beach Resort: Situated near Stone Town, this resort is ideal for those who want to experience both the beach and the historic charm of Zanzibar's capital. With well-maintained gardens, a pool, and easy access to nearby attractions, it's a mid-range gem.

Zanzibar's budget and mid-range accommodations showcase that the island caters to more than just the luxury traveler. These stays, steeped in local flavor and offering genuine hospitality, ensure that every visitor, regardless of budget, can capture the essence of Zanzibar in its fullest form. Whether you're waking up to the sound of waves in a beach bungalow or exploring the alleyways of Stone Town from a cozy inn, Zanzibar welcomes all with open arms and myriad options.

CHAPTER 7

Activities and Adventures

No journey is complete without a dash of adventure and a sprinkle of exhilarating activities. Whether it's scaling mountain peaks, diving into the azure depths of the sea, or exploring the unknown terrains, activities and adventures are what transform a trip from ordinary to extraordinary. Let's delve into the myriad options that beckon the wanderer in search of thrill and excitement.

Snorkeling and Diving Spots

Zanzibar, a mesmerizing archipelago off the coast of Tanzania, is not just about its historical Stone Town and pristine beaches. Beneath the azure waters of the Indian Ocean, Zanzibar harbors a rich marine ecosystem that makes it a favorite among snorkelers and divers. Here's a guide to the best underwater spots in this "Spice Island".

1. Mnemba Atoll: Often deemed Zanzibar's top diving and snorkeling spot, Mnemba Atoll is a protected marine reserve. Its clear turquoise waters are home to diverse coral species, colorful reef fish, and even the occasional dolphin. The atoll's shallow waters are perfect for beginners, while its deeper outer reefs entice seasoned divers.

2. Nungwi and Kendwa Reefs: Located on the northern tip of Zanzibar, these neighboring areas offer excellent snorkeling opportunities. The vibrant coral formations house a myriad of marine species, from parrotfish to moray eels.

3. Kizimkazi: Known for its resident dolphin populations, Kizimkazi on the southern coast is a fantastic spot for both snorkeling and dolphin watching. The playful bottlenose and spinner dolphins often approach boats, offering an exhilarating experience.

4. Tumbatu Island: Just off the northwest coast of Unguja (Zanzibar's main island), Tumbatu is renowned for its pristine reefs. The waters here are teeming with marine life, including rays, nudibranchs, and schools of tropical fish.

5. Pemba Island: A lesser-visited gem in the Zanzibar Archipelago, Pemba Island offers diving spots that are both untouched and diverse. The steep coral walls, clear waters, and abundant marine life make it a dream destination for divers. Popular sites include Fundu Gap and Mesali Island.

6. Leven Bank: Located between Zanzibar and mainland Tanzania, this underwater mount is a hotspot for pelagic species. The currents here bring in barracuda, trevally, and even sharks, making it an exhilarating dive for those seeking a bit of adventure.

7. Bawe Island: Close to Stone Town, Bawe offers both coral gardens for snorkelers and deeper dive sites for scuba enthusiasts. Its accessible location and rich marine life make it a favorite among visitors.

8. Stone Town Reef: While Stone Town is famed for its history and architecture, just offshore lies a delightful snorkeling spot. Perfect for those on a tight schedule, the reef here boasts a variety of corals and fish species.

Zanzibar's underwater realm is a testament to the island's natural wealth. From its vibrant corals to its diverse inhabitants, the marine world here invites visitors to don their fins and masks and plunge into an aquatic paradise. Whether you're a novice snorkeler or a dive master, Zanzibar promises an underwater escapade that will linger in your memories long after you've emerged from its blue depths.

Sailing and Boat Tours

The allure of Zanzibar isn't just limited to its golden beaches and rich history. The surrounding waters of the Indian Ocean beckon visitors to experience the island from a unique vantage point: aboard a sailing vessel. From traditional dhow cruises to exhilarating speedboat tours, Zanzibar's maritime offerings are as varied as they are captivating. Let's set sail through the best sailing and boat tour options the archipelago has to offer.

1. Traditional Dhow Cruises: Dhows, age-old wooden sailing vessels, are emblematic of Zanzibar's maritime heritage. These boats, with their distinctive triangular sails, offer a serene way to explore the surrounding waters. Sunset cruises are particularly popular, where the golden hues of the setting sun paint a magical picture against the azure backdrop of the ocean.

2. Dolphin Tours in Kizimkazi: Head to the southern coast of Zanzibar to the village of Kizimkazi for a boat tour that promises close encounters with playful dolphins. Whether you choose a motorboat or a dhow, spotting these graceful creatures in their natural habitat is an experience to cherish.

3. Sandbank Picnics: Several tour operators offer trips to Zanzibar's pristine sandbanks. These excursions typically include a boat ride to a secluded sandbank where visitors can bask in the sun, snorkel in the clear waters, and relish a beachside picnic before heading back.

4. Blue Safari: This full-day boat excursion takes visitors to explore some of Zanzibar's lesser-known islands and marine sanctuaries. Snorkeling, beachcombing, and savoring a seafood barbecue on a deserted island are highlights of this tour.

5. Fishing Trips: Zanzibar's rich marine ecosystem makes it a hotspot for fishing enthusiasts. Join a deep-sea fishing expedition aboard a well-equipped boat, with opportunities to catch species like marlin, tuna, and sailfish.

6. Pemba Channel Excursions: Pemba Island, part of the Zanzibar Archipelago, is surrounded by deep channels that are teeming with marine life. Sailing tours here often include diving and snorkeling stops, offering a comprehensive oceanic experience.

7. Historical Stone Town Waterfront Cruise: Experience the historic charm of Stone Town from the water. This boat tour offers a different perspective of the UNESCO World Heritage site, highlighting its coastal forts, palaces, and the bustling harbor.

8. Mnemba Atoll Day Trips: Located off the northeast coast of Unguja, Mnemba Atoll is a marine conservation area. Boat tours to this region promise pristine snorkeling sites, encounters with turtles, and a glimpse of the exclusive Mnemba Island.

CHAPTER 8

Local Cuisine and Dining

Zanzibar, fondly known as the Spice Island, boasts a culinary landscape as rich and diverse as its history. A melting pot of African, Arab, Indian, and European influences, Zanzibar's cuisine tantalizes the palate with its exotic flavors, aromatic spices, and fresh ingredients. Whether you're dining in a bustling local market or an elegant beachfront restaurant, the island promises a gastronomic adventure.

Famous Zanzibari Dishes

Zanzibar, with its strategic position along historic trade routes and its rich tapestry of cultures, has cultivated a unique and tantalizing cuisine. Drawing influences from African, Arab, Indian, and Persian kitchens, Zanzibari food is a symphony of flavors and textures. Let's delve into some of the iconic dishes that define the culinary identity of this island paradise.

1. Biryani & Pilau: A nod to its Indian and Persian influences, Zanzibari biryani is a fragrant rice dish layered with spiced meat (chicken, beef, or seafood), and garnished with fried onions and boiled eggs. Pilau, on the other hand, is a one-pot dish where the meat and rice are cooked together with spices like cloves, cardamom, and black pepper, resulting in a delicious, aromatic meal.

2. Urojo (Zanzibar Mix): This tantalizing street food soup combines various elements, including bhajias (deep-fried potato balls), mishkaki (meat skewers), cassava crisps, and hard-boiled eggs, all doused in a tangy, spicy mango broth.

3. Zanzibari Pizza: A distinct entity from its Italian namesake, this is essentially a stuffed pancake. Fillings vary widely, encompassing minced meat and vegetables, cheese, and even sweet options like chocolate or bananas.

4. Mkate wa Ufuta: A sesame bread which is both sweet and savory. It is a popular breakfast item but can be enjoyed at any time of the day, often accompanied by chai (tea).

5. Octopus Curry: A testament to Zanzibar's rich marine offerings, this dish features tender octopus simmered in a rich, spiced coconut gravy.

6. Mandazi: Often referred to as the "Swahili doughnut", these deep-fried dough balls are lightly sweetened and sometimes spiced with cardamom. Perfect with a cup of tea in the morning or as a snack.

7. Kashata: These are flavorful nutty treats made predominantly from coconut or peanuts, combined with sugar and sometimes flavored with cardamom or cinnamon.

8. Wali wa Nazi: A staple in many Zanzibari meals, this is rice cooked in creamy coconut milk, often paired with rich curries or stews.

9. Samaki wa Kupaka: This dish consists of fish (typically kingfish or tuna) that's marinated in a mix of spices, garlic, and lime, then grilled to perfection and served with a coconut-based sauce.

10. Vitumbua: These are sweet, rice-based cakey doughnuts. They have a golden exterior and a soft, fluffy inside, often spiced with cardamom and sprinkled with desiccated coconut.

To truly understand Zanzibar, one must indulge in its cuisine. Each dish tells a story of trade, colonization, migration, and daily life on the island. They encapsulate the essence of Zanzibar – a blend of traditions and cultures, creating a symphony of flavors that dance on the palate.

Top Restaurants and Eateries

Zanzibar isn't just renowned for its pristine beaches and rich history; it's also a gastronomic paradise. A harmonious blend of African, Arab, Indian, and European influences, the island's culinary scene is diverse and tantalizing. For those looking to savor the best of Zanzibari cuisine, here's a curated list of top restaurants and eateries:

1. The Rock Restaurant: Perched on a rock in the turquoise waters of the Indian Ocean, this iconic restaurant offers stunning views and a seafood-centric menu. Their Rock Special, a delicious blend of lobster, jumbo prawns, calamari, and fish, is a must-try.

2. Emerson Spice Tea House Restaurant: Located atop the Emerson Spice Hotel in Stone Town, this rooftop eatery offers panoramic views of the city and ocean. Their daily-changing multi-course tasting menu is an exploration of Zanzibari flavors.

3. Forodhani Gardens: Not a single restaurant, but a bustling evening food market in Stone Town. Here, you can savor local delights such as Zanzibari pizzas, fresh seafood skewers, and sugarcane juice, all at wallet-friendly prices.

4. Lukmaan Restaurant: A legendary eatery in Stone Town, Lukmaan serves traditional Swahili dishes, from biryanis to rich meat stews. Don't miss their delicious juices and desserts.

5. Taperia: Located in the heart of Stone Town, Taperia combines the flavors of Spain and Zanzibar. Alongside traditional tapas, you can also find dishes infused with local spices and ingredients.

6. Zanzibar Coffee House: A café-cum-hotel, it's the place to indulge in freshly brewed Zanzibari coffee paired with delightful pastries or breakfast options. Their rooftop offers splendid views of Stone Town.

7. Coral Rock Café: Located in Jambiani, this restaurant boasts an enviable location with views of the Indian Ocean. Serving a blend of local and international dishes, the fresh seafood options here are particularly commendable.

8. Beach House Restaurant: Situated in Kendwa, this beachfront eatery offers a mix of Zanzibari and Mediterranean dishes. The relaxed ambiance, combined with the sound of the waves, makes for a perfect dining experience.

9. Upendo: Overlooking the famed Rock Restaurant from the Pingwe Beach, Upendo offers a fusion of international dishes with a Zanzibari twist. Their infinity pool and lounge area are perfect for a leisurely meal.

10. Warere Town House Café: Located in Stone Town, this cozy café is known for its delicious breakfast offerings, from omelets to fresh fruits and pastries.

Zanzibar's dining scene reflects its multicultural history and its bounty of fresh produce from land and sea. From elegant rooftop restaurants to bustling local markets, every eatery offers a unique flavor and experience, ensuring that your culinary journey through the island is as memorable as its sunsets and beaches.

Street Food and Local Delights

Zanzibar, with its rich cultural mosaic and historic significance, also shines as a gastronomic star. Away from the confines of fancy restaurants, the streets of Zanzibar come alive with tantalizing aromas and vibrant stalls, promising a culinary adventure that's both authentic and affordable. Let's embark on a flavorful journey, exploring the best of Zanzibari street food and local delights.

1. Zanzibari Pizza: A far cry from its Italian counterpart, the Zanzibari pizza is more like a stuffed pancake or crepe. With fillings ranging from minced meat, vegetables, and cheese to sweet options like banana and chocolate, it's versatile and utterly delicious.

2. Mishkaki: Zanzibar's answer to skewered meat, mishkaki are tender chunks of marinated meat (often beef or chicken) grilled over charcoal, resembling kebabs.

3. Urojo (Zanzibar Mix): This tangy soup is a delightful mishmash of ingredients. Expect chunks of bhajias (fried potato balls), mishkaki, kachori (spiced balls), and sometimes even samosas, all doused in a spicy, tangy broth.

4. Coconut Bean Soup: A hearty and flavorful dish, this soup combines creamy coconut milk with beans, spices, and sometimes chunks of meat or fish.

5. Bhajia: Deep-fried potato balls that are crispy on the outside and soft inside, often seasoned with spices and served with a side of tamarind or coconut chutney.

6. Samosa: These deep-fried triangular pastries are stuffed with a variety of fillings, from spiced meat to lentils and vegetables.

7. Sugar Cane Juice: Refreshing and sweet, freshly squeezed sugar cane juice is a popular drink, often flavored with ginger and lime.

8. Mandazi: Dubbed the 'Swahili doughnut', mandazi are sweet, deep-fried dough balls, lightly spiced with cardamom.

9. Vitumbua: These are sweet rice cake doughnuts, often infused with coconut and cardamom, offering a delightful taste and spongy texture.

10. Seafood Skewers: Given its coastal location, Zanzibar boasts an array of fresh seafood. At street stalls, you can find skewers of fresh fish, octopus, and prawns, grilled to perfection.

11. Kachori: A deep-fried ball made of lentils and flavored with spices, kachori is both crunchy and spicy, making it a favorite snack among locals and tourists alike.

12. Tandai: This unique Zanzibari drink is made by blending spices like ginger, cardamom, and cinnamon with water. The result is a spicy, invigorating drink that's perfect for quenching thirst on a hot day.

A stroll through Zanzibar's bustling markets and alleyways reveals a culinary world where traditions from Africa, the Middle East, and India converge. Every bite tells a story of the island's rich history, its trading past, and its diverse influences. To truly experience Zanzibar, one must indulge in its street food, embracing the flavors that capture the essence of this enchanting island.

CHAPTER 9

Souvenirs and Shopping

Zanzibar, with its rich tapestry of cultures, history, and natural beauty, is not just a destination for relaxation and exploration but also a shopper's paradise. The winding alleyways of Stone Town, the bustling local markets, and the quaint shops offer an array of treasures that capture the essence of this enchanting island. Here's a guide to the must-buy souvenirs and shopping hubs in Zanzibar.

Popular Local Crafts

The rich cultural heritage and diverse history of Zanzibar are beautifully encapsulated in its local crafts. These crafts, deeply rooted in tradition yet reflecting various influences from across the seas, are a testament to the island's artistic prowess and its blend of African, Arab, Indian, and European heritages. Let's delve into the popular local crafts that are the pride of Zanzibar.

1. Zanzibari Doors: Recognized worldwide for their intricate designs and grandeur, Zanzibari doors are hand-carved wooden masterpieces. Adorned with detailed motifs, brass studs, and sometimes even intricate Arabic scripts, these doors are a symbolic representation of the owner's social and economic status.

2. Tinga Tinga Paintings: Originating from Tanzania, the Tinga Tinga art style is vibrant and captivating. These paintings, characterized by their bold colors and whimsical depictions of animals and daily life, are a popular craft in Zanzibar.

3. Soapstone Carvings: Skilled artisans sculpt soapstone, a soft and easily carvable stone, into various shapes and objects. From decorative figurines and bowls to jewelry, soapstone carvings are a testament to the artisan's dexterity and creativity.

4. Beadwork: Zanzibari beadwork, influenced by the Maasai tribe, is both intricate and colorful. Necklaces, bracelets, belts, and other adornments crafted using tiny beads are popular among both locals and tourists.

5. Kanga & Kitenge Fabrics: These traditional textiles are versatile and vibrant. The Kanga often bears Swahili sayings, while the Kitenge comes adorned with bold patterns and prints. They can be worn as garments, used as home furnishings, or even framed as decorative pieces.

6. Basketry: Crafted from locally sourced palm leaves and grasses, Zanzibari baskets are renowned for their durability and intricate patterns. They come in various sizes and designs, from small trinket holders to large storage baskets.

7. Wood Carvings: Beyond the famous doors, Zanzibari artisans showcase their skills in various wooden items such as bowls, furniture, masks, and figurines, often adorned with intricate designs and patterns.

8. Handmade Jewelry: Reflecting the island's fusion of cultures, Zanzibari jewelry ranges from traditional Maasai bead necklaces to silver ornaments influenced by Arabic designs.

9. Coconut Palm Products: The abundant coconut palms in Zanzibar lead to a range of crafts, including coir ropes, mats, and decorative items, all made from different parts of the coconut palm.

10. Traditional Musical Instruments: Instruments like the "taarab" (a type of local lyre) and African drums are handcrafted in Zanzibar, echoing the island's rich musical traditions.

Venturing into the bustling markets and artisanal workshops of Zanzibar, one gets a firsthand experience of the island's crafts heritage. These crafts not only offer a unique memento for visitors but also support the local economy and help keep age-old traditions alive. Whether it's the rhythmic beat of a handmade drum, the vibrant swirls of a Tinga Tinga painting, or the delicate pattern of a hand-woven basket, Zanzibar's crafts capture the heart and soul of the island.

Markets and Shopping Areas

A trip to Zanzibar is as much a sensory experience as it is a historical and beach holiday. Amidst its narrow alleyways, historic ruins, and pristine beaches, Zanzibar offers a delightful shopping experience that's vibrant, diverse, and deeply rooted in its multicultural heritage. Here's a guide to the must-visit markets and shopping areas in Zanzibar:

1. Forodhani Gardens Night Market: As dusk descends on Stone Town, the Forodhani Gardens transform into a bustling food market. Here, you can savor Zanzibari pizzas, fresh seafood skewers, sugarcane juice, and a variety of local snacks.

2. Darajani Bazaar: Often referred to as the "Darajani Market", this is Stone Town's main market. It's a vibrant spot where locals shop for fresh produce, spices, seafood, and meats. The adjoining streets also have shops selling fabric, household items, and souvenirs.

3. Gizenga Street: Located in Stone Town, this street is lined with quaint shops and boutiques selling antiques, jewelry, local crafts, and artworks.

4. Kiponda Street: Another gem in Stone Town, Kiponda Street is known for its traditional shops selling everything from Zanzibari fabrics (Kanga and Kitenge) to local spices.

5. Memories of Zanzibar: This two-storied shop in Stone Town is a one-stop destination for quality souvenirs, ranging from local crafts and jewelry to books and home decor.

6. Zanzibar Curio Shop: Located near the Old Fort, it's a treasure trove of curios, including Tinga Tinga paintings,

Maasai beadwork, wooden carvings, and traditional textiles.

7. The Shangani Craft Market: This outdoor market, situated in Stone Town's Shangani area, is a hub for local artisans to showcase their crafts, from colorful baskets and woodwork to handcrafted jewelry.

8. Kidichi Spice Farms: While Zanzibar boasts several spice farms, Kidichi is one of the oldest and most renowned. Here, you can embark on a guided tour to learn about the island's spices and purchase fresh, locally-grown spices.

9. Jaws Corner: An iconic spot in Stone Town, Jaws Corner is not just a socializing point but also a place where vendors sell antiques, paintings, and other trinkets.

10. Kendwa Beach Market: Located in the northern region of Zanzibar, the Kendwa Beach Market is perfect for picking up beachwear, handmade jewelry, and local crafts.

Zanzibar's shopping areas and markets offer a rich tapestry of local goods, crafts, and flavors. Whether you're a seasoned shopper hunting for unique souvenirs or a traveler keen on experiencing local culture and flavors, Zanzibar's markets promise a delightful and authentic experience. As you browse through the stalls, haggle with vendors, and soak in the vibrant ambiance, you not only take home a piece of Zanzibar but also etched memories of a unique shopping escapade.

CHAPTER 10

Nightlife and Entertainment

Beyond its sun-kissed beaches, historical sites, and vibrant markets, Zanzibar offers a lively nightlife and entertainment scene that caters to diverse tastes. While it's not the bustling nightclub capital of the world, the island has its own serene and unique brand of nighttime fun. Let's explore the array of nighttime attractions and entertainment options that Zanzibar has to offer.

Best Bars and Clubs

Zanzibar might be best known for its pristine beaches and rich history, but as the sun sets, the island reveals a vibrant nightlife. From tranquil beach bars to energetic clubs, there's something for every nocturnal traveler. Here's a round-up of the best bars and clubs to explore in Zanzibar:

1. The Rock Bar, Park Hyatt: Situated in Stone Town, The Rock Bar offers an elegant setting with panoramic views of the dhow-filled harbor and Indian Ocean. It's the perfect spot to unwind with a signature cocktail as the sun dips below the horizon.

2. Cheetah's Rock Bar: Located in Nungwi, this bar is a magnet for backpackers and travelers looking to enjoy a drink, good music, and the occasional party night.

3. Kendwa Rocks: Famous for its monthly full-moon parties, Kendwa Rocks, located in Kendwa Beach, is a must-visit. With beach bonfires, live music, and DJs, it promises an unforgettable night.

4. Cholo's Disco & Bar: As one of the few proper discos on the island, Cholo's in Nungwi becomes the epicenter of

Zanzibar's nightlife during the weekends. The club pulses with a mix of international and Swahili beats.

5. 6 Degrees South Grill and Wine Bar: In the heart of Stone Town, this establishment stands out with its sophisticated ambiance, extensive wine list, and rooftop views.

6. Livingstone Beach Bar: Another gem in Stone Town, it's the ideal place to relish sundowners, with the Indian Ocean stretching out before you and the tunes of live Taarab or local bands setting the mood.

7. Red Monkey Lodge's Bar: Located in Jambiani, this bar offers a laid-back atmosphere with its weekly jam sessions where local musicians and visitors create a musical mosaic.

8. Coral Rock Bar: Nestled in Jambiani, it's a great spot to enjoy a drink with a side of mesmerizing ocean views. The bar occasionally hosts live music and dance performances, enhancing the coastal charm.

9. Tatu Bar at Paje by Night: In Paje, Tatu Bar is the go-to place for those seeking a lively night. Known for its themed nights and DJ events, it's a hub of energy and excitement.

10. Gerry's Bar and Restaurant: Situated in Nungwi, this beachfront bar is perfect for those looking to enjoy a drink with their feet in the sand. The relaxed vibe, complemented by the sound of waves and good music, makes for an idyllic evening.

Zanzibar's nightlife is a blend of its multicultural influences and the tranquil beauty of the island. Whether you're seeking a quiet evening with a cocktail, looking to dance the night away, or eager to soak in live local performances, Zanzibar's bars and clubs promise an array of experiences, making every night a memorable one.

Cultural Shows and Performances

Zanzibar, a melting pot of African, Arab, Indian, and European cultures, offers an array of cultural experiences that transcend its golden beaches and historic structures. Among the most immersive ways to get acquainted with the island's multifaceted heritage is through its cultural shows and performances. These artistic expressions narrate tales of the island's past, its traditions, and the daily lives of its inhabitants.

1. Taarab Music Performances: Unique to the coastal regions of East Africa, Taarab music is a harmonious blend of Swahili tunes, African rhythms, and Arab melodies. These performances, often accompanied by dramatic vocals and traditional instruments like the oud (lute) and qanun (zither), can be enjoyed at various venues across Zanzibar, especially in Stone Town.

2. Ngoma Drum and Dance: This traditional African dance and drum show is a powerful and energetic performance that narrates various stories and events. The rhythm of the drums, combined with the expressive dance moves, makes for a captivating experience.

3. Dhow Musical Shows: Celebrating Zanzibar's maritime history, these performances occur on traditional dhows (wooden sailing vessels) and include a mix of music, dance, and tales of the seafaring past.

4. Fire Dancing at Kendwa Rocks: One of the most mesmerizing performances you can witness, fire dancers at Kendwa Beach perform intricate routines, juggling and dancing with flaming torches against the backdrop of the setting sun.

5. Swahili Storytelling: Dive deep into the folklore and myths of Zanzibar through its traditional storytelling sessions. These narratives, often peppered with moral lessons and historical tales, offer a deeper understanding of the island's cultural fabric.

6. Capoeira Shows: Reflecting the influence of Brazilian settlers and the broader African diaspora, capoeira performances in Zanzibar combine martial arts, dance, and music into a fluid and fascinating display.

7. Zanzibar International Film Festival (ZIFF): While primarily a film festival, ZIFF also showcases various cultural performances, including music, dance, and theater, highlighting the rich tapestry of Zanzibari and East African arts.

8. Mwaka Kogwa Festival: Held in Makunduchi, this annual event celebrates the Persian New Year. Apart from the ritualistic mock fights, the festival includes vibrant music and dance performances that showcase the island's Persian influences.

9. Traditional Puppet Shows: A unique form of entertainment, these puppet shows often depict daily life scenarios, historical events, or folktales, providing both entertainment and insights into local traditions.

Zanzibar's cultural shows and performances offer travelers an authentic and engaging means to connect with the island's heart and soul. They reflect the rhythms, stories, and passions of its people, ensuring that visitors take away memories that resonate far beyond the island's sandy shores and turquoise waters.

Night Markets

The allure of Zanzibar isn't limited to its daytime charm. As the sun sets, the island takes on a whole new persona, especially evident in its vibrant night markets. A whirl of colors, tantalizing aromas, and the cheerful cacophony of vendors and shoppers, these markets offer a sensory-rich experience and a genuine taste of Zanzibar's local life.

1. Forodhani Gardens Night Market:

Perhaps the most iconic of all Zanzibar's night markets, the Forodhani Gardens in Stone Town transforms into a bustling food bazaar each evening. With the Indian Ocean as its backdrop, the market boasts a vast array of stalls offering delicacies such as Zanzibari pizzas, fresh seafood skewers, urojo (local soup), sugarcane juice with ginger and lime, and a plethora of grilled meats and local desserts. The market is not only a haven for foodies but also a vibrant spot to observe local life and mingle with residents.

2. Darajani Bazaar's Evening Vendors:

While Darajani is a hive of activity during the day, its evening avatar has a distinct charm. Some food vendors and stalls continue into the night, offering fresh produce, local snacks, and an array of spices that Zanzibar is famed for.

3. Jaws Corner:

A socializing point by day, Jaws Corner in Stone Town becomes a modest night market spot where locals gather for coffee, local tea, and casual conversations. Street food vendors also set up nearby, adding to the ambience with their offerings.

4. Paje Night Market:

For those stationed on the eastern coast of Zanzibar, Paje's night market offers a delightful mix of local dishes, fresh fruits, and occasionally, craft items. It's smaller in scale compared to Forodhani but exudes a quaint charm.

5. Kendwa Beach Night Stalls:

Post sunset, the beaches of Kendwa, especially near popular resorts, see a smattering of stalls offering local handicrafts, jewelry, and trinkets. Though not a 'market' in the traditional sense, it's a great spot for nighttime shopping under the stars.

6. Michenzani Local Night Market:

Away from the main tourist areas, the Michenzani neighborhood in Stone Town has its own local night market. It offers a more authentic experience, predominantly catering to the locals. Here, one can find an array of local foods, fresh produce, and daily essentials.

Venturing into Zanzibar's night markets provides travelers with an authentic experience, far removed from the structured itineraries of daytime sightseeing. The markets capture the island's pulsating heart, its culinary richness, and the warm spirit of its people. So, whether you're looking to satiate your palate, hunt for local crafts, or simply soak in the nocturnal vibes of Zanzibar, the night markets await with open arms and myriad offerings.

CHAPTER 11

Getting Around Zanzibar

Zanzibar, an archipelago off the Tanzanian coast, boasts a blend of pristine beaches, rich history, and vibrant local culture. While the islands are relatively compact, knowing the best modes of transport can enhance your travel experience, allowing you to explore Zanzibar's myriad offerings seamlessly.

Public Transport Options

Zanzibar, with its blend of rich cultural heritage and breathtaking landscapes, offers visitors a myriad of experiences. For the intrepid traveler keen on truly immersing themselves in the local vibe, understanding and using public transport can be both cost-effective and enriching. Let's delve into the various public transport options available in Zanzibar:

1. Dala-Dala:
These are the lifeline of Zanzibar's public transport system. Dala-dalas are either minibuses or converted trucks with

wooden benches. Each vehicle typically has a route name or number written on the front, indicating its destination. They operate from early morning till late evening, and while they don't follow a strict schedule, they're relatively frequent. The main dala-dala station in Stone Town is the Darajani Market, but you'll find stops throughout the island.

Pros:

- Extremely affordable.
- Provides a genuine local experience.

Cons:

- Can be crowded, especially during peak hours.
- Limited comfort due to the rustic nature of the vehicles.

2. Shared Taxis:

In some areas, especially when dala-dalas are infrequent, shared taxis become an alternative. They're standard cars, accommodating multiple passengers headed in the same direction.

Pros:

- More comfortable than dala-dalas.
- Reasonably priced, especially when splitting the cost.

Cons:

- Slightly more expensive than dala-dalas.
- Need to negotiate fares in advance.

3. Ferries:

For those looking to travel between Zanzibar's main island, Unguja, and its sister island, Pemba, or smaller surrounding islands, public ferries are available. These vessels range from smaller boats to larger ships, with the latter being more comfortable and faster.

Pros:

- Efficient way to travel between islands.
- Offers scenic views during the journey.

Cons:

- Can be crowded.
- Weather-dependent; rough seas might lead to cancellations.

4. Boda-Boda (Motorbike Taxis):

These are motorcycles that can be hailed for short distances, especially in areas where taxis or dala-dalas are sparse.

Pros:

- Quick for short distances.
- Can navigate through traffic or narrow roads.

Cons:

- Safety concerns; helmets might not always be provided.
- Not ideal for long distances or for those with a lot of luggage.

5. Bicycle Taxis:

In certain parts of Zanzibar, especially in more rural areas or smaller villages, bicycle taxis are an option. They're essentially bicycles with a padded seat or carrier on the back.

Pros:

- Eco-friendly.
- Suitable for very short distances.

Cons:

- Limited to areas with less traffic.
- Can be uncomfortable for longer rides.

Tips for Using Public Transport in Zanzibar:

Always agree on a fare beforehand to avoid overcharging.

For safety, especially on boda-bodas, ensure the vehicle is in good condition and, if possible, use a helmet.

While using dala-dalas, keep personal belongings secure as these vehicles can get crowded.

Embracing Zanzibar's public transport not only eases your travel but also offers a window into the daily rhythms of local life. As you journey through the island's winding roads, the colorful tapestry of Zanzibar unfolds, making each trip a unique adventure in itself.

Car Rentals and Driving Tips

Zanzibar, with its blend of historical charm and stunning natural beauty, offers a plethora of attractions for travelers to explore. For those keen on discovering the island at their own pace, renting a car can be an ideal option. Car rentals in Zanzibar cater to a range of needs and budgets, ensuring that visitors can roam freely, from the winding streets of Stone Town to the remote corners of the island.

Several reputable car rental agencies operate out of Zanzibar, many of which are conveniently located at the Abeid Amani Karume International Airport and in Stone Town. These agencies offer a variety of vehicles, from compact cars suitable for city exploration to sturdy 4x4s that can handle the more rugged terrains of the island. It's advisable to book in advance, especially during peak tourist seasons, to ensure availability and competitive rates.

Driving in Zanzibar can be a unique experience. The island follows left-hand driving, and while the main roads are in reasonably good condition, some rural areas might offer more challenging terrains. It's essential to be cautious of potholes, pedestrians, cyclists, and the occasional livestock crossing the road. Moreover, road signs can be sparse in certain areas, so having a reliable map or GPS is beneficial.

For those unfamiliar with the local driving customs, hiring a car with a local driver can be a great alternative. Not only does this ensure safe navigation through Zanzibar's roads, but local drivers often double up as informal guides, providing insights and recommendations that might not be found in guidebooks.

To rent a car in Zanzibar, you'll typically need a valid driving license from your home country, and some agencies might also ask for an International Driving Permit. It's crucial to ensure that the rental includes comprehensive insurance to cover potential damages or accidents.

Parking in Stone Town can be challenging due to its narrow streets and limited spaces. However, most hotels and resorts outside Stone Town offer ample parking space. When venturing into the city or popular tourist spots, consider using designated parking areas or seek advice on safe parking locations.

Lastly, while the freedom of having a rental car is unparalleled, always prioritize safety. Avoid driving at night, especially outside Stone Town, as the roads are not well-lit and can pose challenges even for experienced drivers. With a rented vehicle at your disposal, the enchanting landscapes, hidden beaches, and vibrant villages of Zanzibar await your discovery, ensuring a journey filled with memories and adventures.

Walking and Cycling Paths

Zanzibar, a picturesque archipelago, is not just about pristine beaches and historical relics. The island offers an array of trails and paths that allow travelers to delve deeper into its beauty at a leisurely pace. Walking and cycling are not only eco-friendly ways to explore but also provide intimate encounters with the island's landscapes and culture.

Walking Paths:

Stone Town Heritage Walks: The maze-like alleys of Stone Town are best explored on foot. Each turn reveals a piece of history, from ornate doors to ancient ruins. A guided heritage walk can provide insights into the town's rich past and architectural wonders.

Jozani Forest Trails: This is Zanzibar's prime conservation area and offers marked trails through the lush forest. Walking here can lead to sightings of the endemic Red Colobus Monkeys, vibrant bird species, and a variety of plant life.

Nungwi Village Walks: Beyond its beautiful beaches, a stroll through Nungwi village unveils the local way of life, fishing traditions, and boat-building yards.

Spice Plantation Tours: Walking through the island's spice plantations is both educational and aromatic. These guided walks offer firsthand encounters with the plants and processes that have made Zanzibar the "Spice Island."

Cycling Paths:

Stone Town to Paje: This route, though requiring a bit of stamina, rewards cyclists with varied landscapes. From the urban charm of Stone Town, the journey progresses through local villages, farmlands, and finally, the pristine beaches of Paje.

Kizimkazi Village Tour: Starting from the village, this cycling route explores the southern coast of Zanzibar, including the famous Dolphin Bay.

Jambiani Coastal Ride: Jambiani, with its turquoise waters and white sands, offers a serene cycling experience. The path is relatively flat, making it suitable even for novice cyclists.

Matemwe to Mnemba Island: For the adventurous, this cycling path combines both land and sea. Cyclists can ride through the fishing village of Matemwe and then opt for a canoe ride to the private Mnemba Island.

Several resorts and tour operators in Zanzibar offer bike rentals, complete with helmets and maps. For those unfamiliar with the terrains, guided cycling tours are available, ensuring safety and a richer understanding of the regions explored.

When embarking on walking or cycling excursions, it's essential to be prepared. Wear comfortable clothing, sturdy shoes, and always carry water. Sunscreen and hats are a must, given the tropical climate of Zanzibar. Additionally, respecting local customs, especially in more conservative villages, is crucial. Opting for modest clothing and seeking permission before photographing people or their properties is advisable.

Walking and cycling in Zanzibar are not just modes of transport; they're windows into the soul of the island. Whether it's the rhythmic footsteps on a forest trail, the wind against your face as you cycle along the coast, or the spontaneous interactions with locals.

CHAPTER 12

Practical Information

Venturing to Zanzibar offers a mesmerizing blend of turquoise waters, rich history, and cultural experiences. However, to make your journey smooth and enjoyable, it's essential to arm yourself with some practical information.

Vaccinations and Health Precautions

Embarking on a journey to Zanzibar is a thrilling experience, blending beach relaxation with rich cultural exploration. However, as with any travel, it's essential to prioritize your health. Below are the necessary vaccinations and health precautions you should consider when traveling to Zanzibar:

1. Vaccinations:

- Yellow Fever: While Zanzibar is not a Yellow Fever endemic area, a proof of vaccination might be required if you're traveling from a country where the disease is

prevalent. Even if not mandatory, it's a recommended vaccine for travelers.
- Typhoid and Hepatitis A: Both can be contracted through contaminated food or water. Considering the varying food and water safety levels in different regions of Zanzibar, these vaccinations are advisable.
- Tetanus, Diphtheria, and Polio: It's essential to ensure you're up-to-date with these routine vaccinations.
- Hepatitis B: Recommended, especially if you plan to have close contact with the local population or are at risk of potential exposure through medical procedures or other means.
- Rabies: Zanzibar has a history of rabies cases. If you plan to be involved in outdoor activities or are likely to come into contact with animals, consider this vaccination.

2. Malaria Precautions:

Zanzibar falls within a malaria zone. Taking antimalarial medication is crucial. Consult your doctor about the best prophylactic for your needs and duration of stay.

- Use mosquito repellents, especially during dawn and dusk when mosquitoes are most active.
- Sleep under a treated mosquito net to further reduce the risk.

3. Food and Water Safety:

- Only drink bottled or boiled water. Avoid tap water, ice cubes, or drinks that might be made from tap water.
- Ensure your food is thoroughly cooked. Opt for hot, freshly prepared foods and avoid raw salads or fruits that can't be peeled.
- Be cautious with street food. While it's a part of the local experience, ensure the food is cooked in hygienic conditions and is still hot when served.

4. Sun and Heat:

Zanzibar's tropical climate means strong sun and high temperatures. Always wear a high SPF sunscreen, and reapply regularly.

- Wear hats, sunglasses, and lightweight long-sleeved clothing to protect against the sun's rays.
- Stay hydrated. Drink plenty of water throughout the day, especially if you're indulging in physical activities.

5. Swimming Precautions:

- While Zanzibar boasts beautiful beaches, be wary of strong currents and tides. Always check the safety of a swimming spot, and if unsure, ask locals or your accommodation for advice.
- Avoid swimming in freshwater sources, as they may be home to parasites.

6. General Precautions:

Always have a well-stocked medical kit, including basics like antiseptics, bandages, painkillers, and any personal medication.

Consider investing in travel insurance that covers medical evacuation, given the limited medical facilities in Zanzibar.

Staying vigilant about your health doesn't mean compromising on the fun. With the right precautions, you can fully immerse yourself in all that Zanzibar has to offer, ensuring that your memories are only of the adventures and beauty of the Spice Island.

Safe Travel Tips

Zanzibar, a paradise archipelago, offers a captivating mix of sandy beaches, cultural heritage, and vibrant local life. While it's a popular and relatively safe destination, being aware of certain travel precautions can ensure a hassle-free experience. Here are some safety tips to keep in mind while exploring the Spice Island:

1. Respect Local Customs:

Zanzibar's population is predominantly Muslim. To show respect:

- Dress modestly, especially when not on the beach. Women should consider wearing dresses or skirts that cover the knees and tops that cover the shoulders.
- Public displays of affection are frowned upon, so it's best to be discreet.
- Be mindful of local traditions, especially during the holy month of Ramadan.

2. Beware of Beach Touts:

While many locals are genuinely friendly, be cautious of beach touts selling goods or services. It's okay to politely decline if you're not interested. Always agree on prices upfront to avoid misunderstandings.

3. Safe Swimming:

Zanzibar's beaches are stunning, but:

- Beware of strong currents. It's best to swim in designated areas.
- Avoid isolated beaches, especially after dark.
- Watch out for sea urchins; their spines can be painful. Wearing water shoes can be a good precaution.

4. Health Precautions:
- Drink only bottled or boiled water.
- Avoid eating raw or undercooked food.
- Use mosquito repellent and sleep under mosquito nets to prevent mosquito-borne diseases.

5. Watch Your Belongings:
- Petty theft can occur, especially in crowded areas like markets. Use a money belt or hidden pouch for valuable items.
- Avoid displaying signs of wealth, like wearing expensive jewelry.
- When at the beach, don't leave your belongings unattended.

6. Night Safety:
- Stone Town is relatively safe, but it's wise to avoid dimly-lit alleyways at night.
- It's best to use a taxi after dark, even for short distances. Ensure it's a reputable taxi service, and negotiate fares in advance.

7. Transport:

- If renting a vehicle, ensure it's in good condition. Remember to drive on the left.
- When using dala-dalas (local buses), be prepared for crowded conditions and keep an eye on your belongings.
- Always negotiate prices before using any form of transport.

8. Avoid Drugs:

Drug possession and use are illegal in Zanzibar and come with severe penalties. Avoid any involvement, even if approached with offers.

9. Stay Updated:

- It's always a good idea to check your country's travel advisories for Zanzibar before your trip.
- Familiarize yourself with local emergency numbers and know the location of the nearest hospital or medical facility.

10. Trust Your Instincts:

If something feels off, it probably is. Trusting your gut can be one of the best safety measures.

Traveling to Zanzibar is a dream for many, and with a touch of awareness and preparation, it can be an unforgettable experience filled with awe-inspiring sights and rich cultural exchanges. Embrace the beauty of Zanzibar with an open heart, but always with a touch of caution, ensuring a journey that's as safe as it is spectacular.

Currency and Emergency

Zanzibar, a tropical haven, welcomes visitors with its azure waters and rich cultural tapestry. However, for a smooth and enjoyable trip, it's crucial to understand the local currency nuances and be prepared for any emergencies.

Currency in Zanzibar:

1. Official Currency: The Tanzanian Shilling (TZS) is the official currency of Zanzibar, as the island is part of Tanzania.
2. Using Foreign Currency: US Dollars are widely accepted, especially in hotels, restaurants, and tourist-oriented establishments. However, for smaller

purchases in local markets or remote areas, Tanzanian Shillings are preferable.

3. ATMs: ATMs are available in Stone Town and some major tourist spots. They dispense Tanzanian Shillings. It's advisable to use ATMs attached to banks for security reasons, and always shield your PIN.

4. Currency Exchange: You can exchange foreign currency at banks, hotels, or authorized foreign exchange bureaus in Stone Town. It's recommended to keep a receipt of your transaction, especially if you plan to convert any unused Tanzanian Shillings back to your home currency upon departure.

5. Credit and Debit Cards: Major hotels and some restaurants in Zanzibar accept credit and debit cards, but it's always good to ask beforehand. Visa and Mastercard are the most widely accepted. Note that there might be a service charge for card payments.

6. Tipping: Tipping is appreciated for good service. In restaurants, a tip of around 10% is customary, unless a service charge is already included in the bill. For tour guides, drivers, or hotel staff, tipping is a nice gesture but the amount is at your discretion.

Emergency Information:

1. Police: If you need police assistance, dial 112 or 999. There's also a tourist police unit in Stone Town dedicated to assisting tourists.
2. Medical Emergencies: The main hospital in Zanzibar is the Mnazi Mmoja Hospital in Stone Town. For minor ailments, there are also smaller clinics and pharmacies available. It's recommended to have comprehensive travel insurance that includes medical evacuation, as some severe medical issues might require treatment outside Zanzibar.
3. Lost or Stolen Passports: If your passport is lost or stolen, report it immediately to the local police and then contact your country's embassy or consulate in Tanzania.
4. Natural Disasters: While Zanzibar is relatively safe from major natural disasters, it's good to be aware of seasonal weather patterns, especially if you're visiting during the rainy season. Hotels and local authorities

will provide guidance in case of severe weather conditions.

5. Local Contacts: Always have contact details of your accommodation, a local guide, or a tour operator. They can be invaluable in providing assistance or advice in case of emergencies.

While Zanzibar is a welcoming destination, being informed about currency matters and prepared for potential emergencies ensures a hassle-free and enjoyable stay. Taking a few proactive steps can make all the difference, allowing you to immerse fully in the mesmerizing beauty and culture of the Spice Island.

Conclusion

Zanzibar, often referred to as the 'Spice Island', is more than just a destination; it's a journey into a world where history, culture, and nature merge beautifully. From the architectural wonders of Stone Town to the pristine beaches that hug its coastline, every corner of Zanzibar tells a story. But as with any travel adventure, being prepared and informed is key to fully immersing oneself in the experience. This guide aims to arm travelers with essential insights and tips to navigate Zanzibar seamlessly. Whether you're a history buff, a beach lover, or a culinary explorer, Zanzibar promises memories that linger and experiences that enrich. So, pack your bags, respect the local norms, and embark on a journey to discover the myriad wonders of Zanzibar. Safe travels and let the Spice Island charm you in its unique way!

Printed in Great Britain
by Amazon